Respondin
Ukraine–Russia War

CW01674338

Robert Innes
Bishop of the Diocese in Europe

GROVE BOOKS LIMITED
RIDLEY HALL RD CAMBRIDGE CB3 9HU

Contents

Preface

Following his visit to Ukraine in November/December 2022, the Archbishop of Canterbury requested the Church of England's Faith and Order Commission to produce a short document for the House of Bishops to stimulate reflection and response amongst the bishops, prompted by the various difficult questions raised by the war between Russia and Ukraine. A working group of theologians and those with some particular relevant experience or expertise was formed and met regularly during the first half of 2023 to address the Archbishop's request. The working group comprised: The Rt Revd Dr Robert Innes (Chair of the Faith and Order Commission), The Revd Canon Dr Anderson Jeremiah, Dr Christina Laschenko, Dr Ziya Meral, The Rt Revd Dr Graham Tomlin, Major General Roddy Porter, Dr Charles Reed, The Revd Dr (Wing Commander) David Richardson, The Revd Preb Dr Isabelle Hamley.

This Grove booklet is a slightly longer and different version of the paper that was submitted by the Group to the House of Bishops in July 2023. Because of the great importance of the issues, we were anxious that they receive a wider hearing. Our Group was convinced that the Ukraine war, serious as it is in itself, foregrounds a deeply worrying global context. This booklet is therefore a wake-up call to a church which may be insufficiently attentive to the signs of the times. It also holds before us the reality of an interconnected planet and a neighbourly interdependence which is desperately needed at the same time as it is being weaponized.

The cover image is copyright © Grove Books Ltd

Copyright © Robert Innes 2023

First Impression October 2023
ISSN 1470-854X
ISBN 978 1 78827 345 9

1 Introduction

In 2022 Russia reinvaded Ukraine from the east, north and south in a dramatic ramping up of a conflict which began in 2014. The war is much the most serious conflict in Europe since World War 2 with the destruction of cities such as Mariupol, massacre of civilians in, for example, Bucha, the environmental catastrophe caused by the collapse of the Nova Kakhova dam and the internal and external displacement of many millions of Ukrainian people. Russia's invasion poses a serious threat to the post-1945 rules-based international order.

The impact of this war politically, economically and environmentally means that no country on earth is unaffected by it. Our world is increasingly interdependent, and precisely this interdependence has been weaponized through sanctions, attacks on food production and distribution, and threats against nuclear power plants. Britain has a particular military involvement in this conflict at one remove through the supply of sophisticated weapons and military training.

The war in Ukraine is a prominent feature of a more general and deeply worrying international military arena. Annual military spending across the world has been increasing year on year to reach two trillion dollars. New weapons like hypersonic missiles have been deployed in the Ukraine war. Military drones, which vary from the size of a human hand to a small aircraft, are proliferating and are relatively easy to build. Developments in artificial intelligence are leading to the possibility of increasingly autonomous weapons systems.

Russia is deploying nuclear weapons in Belarus and threatens use of nuclear weapons against Ukraine—albeit that Ukraine gave up its nuclear arsenal in 1994 in exchange for Russian commitments to respect Ukrainian sovereignty and territorial integrity. At the same time, North Korea continues its ballistic missile testing, China plans a threefold increase in its stockpile of nuclear weapons by 2030 and there seems little prospect of reviving key nuclear arms control treaties.

- The world is becoming a very dangerous place. What is the function of the church at this time and how should it respond?

2 Four Perspectives on the Conflict

Perspective from Ukraine

The history of the people and lands of Ukraine is complicated. From the fourteenth to the eighteenth centuries, portions of Ukraine were ruled by Lithuania, Poland and Russia. In addition, Cossacks controlled their own area of territory. Following a period of conflict in the mid-seventeenth century, the Treaty of Andrusovo was concluded in 1667 under which Ukraine was partitioned along the Dneiper River: the west, known as the Right Bank, reverted to Poland, while Russia retained the east, known as the Left Bank, together with Kyiv. Most of Ukraine subsequently fell to Russian rule in the eighteenth century. In the aftermath of World War I and the Russian Revolution of 1917, most of the Ukraine region became a republic of the Soviet Union.

Through much of the twentieth century Ukraine suffered hugely under the Russian empire. During World War I, ethnic Ukrainians, Jews and Poles from Western Ukrainian lands were deported in large numbers. In the interwar period, Ukrainians were badly oppressed by the Bolsheviks with state appropriation of farmland and suppression of peasantry. Most infamously, the man-made Great Famine (Holodomor) from 1932–1933 killed many millions of Ukrainians. During World War II, Ukraine was occupied by the Nazis and suffered immense human and material losses. After that war, hundreds of thousands of real and alleged Nazi collaborators and 'bourgeois nationalists' were sent to Siberian concentration camps. A prolonged and violent Sovietization process continued throughout Stalin's rule.

Conditions improved under Khrushchev (whose wife was born in Ukraine), with growth in Ukrainian confidence and cultural identity, provided that Ukrainians understood their 'junior' status *vis-à-vis* Russia. Nevertheless, contemporary Ukrainian voices understand their history as a 250-year struggle to escape Russian domination, with the twentieth century period between occupation by the Bolsheviks and the collapse of the Soviet Union as 73 years of particularly cruel oppression.

The present conflict is thus informed by a history which is all too present in the memory and experience of Ukrainian families. Indeed, the 2022 invasion is seen by Ukrainians as generating an existential question: is Ukraine 'to be or not to be'? Those who know or meet Ukrainians cannot therefore fail to be impressed by the almost complete sense of resilience and determination to fight. It is clear from many conversations with the inhabitants of Bucha and Irpin, as well as oral testimony from other parts of Ukraine, that this is experienced as a national war of survival in which every section and stratum of society is engaged. There exists a widespread national determination, shared by the Ukrainian diaspora, to succeed at all costs.

Perspective from Moscow

In an article of 12 July 2021, President Putin explains his view of 'the historical unity of Russians and Ukrainians.' Russia and Ukraine are, for Mr Putin, 'parts of what is essentially the same historical and spiritual space.' Putin invokes the notion of Ancient Rus as a territory comprising modern Russia, Byelorussia and Ukraine, bound together by a common language (Old Russian), ties of economy and governance and the Orthodox faith. He describes how the throne of Kiev (sic) held a dominant position in Ancient Rus, which was 'the mother of all Russian cities.' Putin sees the sixteenth and seventtenth centuries as a period of Orthodox (Ukrainian) struggle for liberation from Polish and Lithuanian rule. He notes how the name 'Ukraine' derives from the Old Russian *okraina* (periphery), and the word 'Ukrainian' originally referred to frontier guards who protected the external borders. Putin speaks of the great affection that Russians and Ukrainians feel for each other down to this day and argues the economic prospects of both Ukraine and Russian are better together. Putin therefore sees the assertion of distinct Ukrainian identity linked to independence as historically misguided and as inspired by Western anti-Russian sentiment. 'It would not be an exaggeration to say that the path of forced assimilation, the formation of an ethnically pure Ukrainian state, aggressive towards Russia, is comparable in its consequences to the use of weapons of mass destruction against us.'[1]

Ukraine is seen as a puppet of the West enacting anti-Russian legislation

Following the Euro-Maidan revolution and the installation of a pro-Western president, Ukraine is seen as a puppet of the West enacting anti-Russian legislation. So Russia's military action in Ukraine is directed not just against a hostile Ukrainian regime but against the Western forces backing it.

NATO is experienced by Putin's regime as an anti-Russian alliance, which is seeking ultimately to destroy and break up Russia. 'They have one goal: to disband the former Soviet Union and its fundamental part—the Russian Federation.'[2] NATO is understood to have gone back on an agreement given to Gorbachev in 1990 that it would not expand beyond its current borders.[3] Since then, NATO has grown from 17 to 30 countries, and has steadily expanded east, incorporating the Baltic States, and offering (albeit vague) promises to

Ukraine and Georgia that they would one day be able to join NATO. Mr. Putin holds that NATO represents an existential threat to Russia. 'I do not even know if such an ethnic group as the Russian people will be able to survive in the form in which it exists today.'[4]

These are the official views of President Putin and his regime. Because of the repressive censorship in Russia it is impossible to know how far these views are shared by ordinary Russians. However, we have not seen widespread protest within Russia against this narrative. The clash of the narratives and visions of Ukrainian identity between modern-day Ukraine and Putin's Russia is abundantly clear.

Perspective from the UK

Trading links between Britain and Russia go back to the formation of the Russia Company in the 1550s, a company of Merchant Adventurers who also fostered links between the royal houses. Since then, Britain and Russia have sometimes been allies (against Napoleon and in the two world wars) and sometimes enemies (notably in the 1850s Crimean War). After the ending of the Cold War and the dissolution of the Soviet Union, political and business ties between the two nations flourished. The late Queen Elizabeth II visited Moscow as a guest of President Yeltsin in 1994. This visit led to the handing back of the extensive set of buildings that make up St Andrew's Anglican Church, Moscow. There was the sense that a large, powerful, frequently mysterious and sometimes brutal country (historically represented in political cartoons as a bear) was at last opening itself to the West.

However, more recently relations grew very difficult. There were allegations of Russian interference in American elections and the UK Brexit referendum. The poisoning of Sergei and Yulia Skripal in 2018 in Salisbury—an episode which could have endangered the lives of many innocent people—led to the virtual ending of UK/Russian diplomatic engagement and 28 countries expelling Russian spies acting as diplomats. Following the 2022 invasion, the UK's political and diplomatic relations with Russia ended completely and sanctions are intended to make travel and business contact nearly impossible.

By contrast public sympathy for the plight of Ukraine has been huge. In the face of a generally hostile politics of immigration, there has been much encouragement to welcome and receive Ukrainian migrants. Throughout the country, people have raised Ukrainian flags and welcomed Ukrainians into their homes. Undoubtedly, there were felt resonances with Britain's own World War II experience of holding out against a powerful neighbour. Britain thus became one of the largest donors of humanitarian and financial aid to Ukraine and was the first country in Europe to donate lethal military support.

The costs of the war to UK citizens have been very high. Coming hot on the heels of the COVID-19 pandemic, the Russian invasion of Ukraine caused a surge in oil, gas and food prices. At the start of wars, the price of oil typically surges as countries seek to buy more, but in this case supply was in addition restricted because of sanctions. The Russian invasion and blockade of Ukraine also caused a global shortage of wheat, sunflower oil and maize. Whilst high inflation is likely to be due to other long-term British economic problems (low productivity, poor economic growth, worsened trading prospects due to Brexit), the Ukraine war has both triggered and exacerbated severe increases in the cost of living.

The crisis has been more acute for the poorest UK households, which typically spend a higher proportion of their income on food and fuel costs. There have been many accounts of people having to choose between paying for food or heating, with local churches at the forefront of those providing assistance through food banks or warm places. Those living with disabilities have been particularly badly hit.[5]

Perspective from Global Majority/South Countries

A recent study by the Bennett Institute for Public Policy at the University of Cambridge has found that the war in Ukraine has widened a global divide in attitudes to the US and Russia as well as China.[6] Research into attitudes in 137 countries found that, on the one hand, Western democracies stand more firmly than ever behind the United States. In addition, the war has encouraged upper-income democracies in South America, Asia-Pacific and Eastern Europe to move to a more pro-American stance. However, across a vast span of countries stretching from continental Eurasia to the north and west of Africa, the study finds the opposite: societies have moved closer to Russia and China over the last decade. As a result, China and Russia are now narrowly ahead of the United States in their popularity among developing countries.

One commentator suggests five reasons why the Global South is in general not taking the West's side, namely:

- The Global South does not believe that the West understands or empathizes with its problems.
- Many countries in Latin America, Africa and Asia see the world through the lens of colonialism.
- The war in Ukraine is seen as mainly about the future of Europe rather than the future of the entire world.

- The world economy is no longer dominated by America or led by the West, and the Global South now has other options.
- The 'rules-based international order' [being a liberal Western creation] is losing credibility and is in decline.[7]

In line with this, a UN debate in February 2023 on the war calling for a 'comprehensive, just and lasting peace' exhibited significant differences over how to achieve the envisaged outcome. Western allies of Kyiv were mostly united in condemning Moscow, promising to support Ukraine for as long as necessary and calling for Russia to be held accountable for its crimes. They had no new diplomatic initiative to reveal. By contrast, speakers representing non-Western states were typically more inclined to call for an early, negotiated end to the war. Some made tentative proposals for mechanisms to reach that goal, though with little actionable detail. Many non-Western representatives did not speak at all: a good part of the UN membership preferred to keep a low profile over the war.

As a leading Global South nation, India has sometimes been looked to as a possible mediator in the conflict. Shortly after Russia invaded, the Indian government headed by Prime Minister Modi adopted a policy of studied neutrality. India abstained from the first UN vote demanding an end to the Russian offensive and has kept up this pattern in successive votes. At the same time India, along with China, has been importing record levels of Russian oil since the war began, benefiting from the big cuts in Russian oil and gas prices. The West's failure to gain widespread Global South support means, at least, that the effect of sanctions on Russia has been significantly attenuated. More broadly, the West's liberal democratic and capitalist vision for the world is not one the Global South necessarily shares. India, together with some other Global South nations, shares the quest for a multipolar world not dominated by the monopolar power and values of the US. This is, of course, also a policy objective of Russia.

- Are Global South countries such as India a possible source of hope in the conflict?
- Is multipolarity simply a cloak for the tacit support of authoritarian regimes?
- If support for Ukraine is morally right, what view do we take of those Global South countries who are taking the opportunity to benefit from cheap Russian energy, thereby undermining Western sanctions?

3 Contemporary Warfare and New Questions

The *Bulletin of the Atomic Scientists* reset their famous Doomsday Clock on 24 January 2023 to 90 seconds to midnight, as a sign that the world is closer to catastrophe than ever. The move, which is the closest to widespread calamity humanity has ever been judged to be, was 'largely, though not exclusively' due to the war in Ukraine. Mary Robinson, a former UN High Commissioner for Human Rights, commented, 'The Doomsday Clock is sounding an alarm for the whole of humanity. We are on the brink of a precipice. But our leaders are not acting at sufficient speed or scale to secure a peaceful and livable planet.'[8]

The Doomsday Clock responds to the large-scale threats to humanity, notably nuclear weapons, climate change and biological threats. The 2023 clock reset was attributed largely to the *risk of nuclear escalation* from the Ukraine invasion. Even since January, the situation has become more worrying, with continuing Russian threats to use tactical nuclear weapons and President Putin's February announcement that he would suspend participation in a new START treaty—the last remaining nuclear arms control treaty between the US and Russia. The likelihood that Russia will actually use nuclear weapons probably remains low, but it will nonetheless increase if Russia becomes desperate. As former Russian president Medvedev has said, 'Nuclear powers do not lose major conflicts on which their fate depends.'[9]

The Doomsday Clock reset calculation relates to the increasing use of disruptive technologies

But another part of the Doomsday Clock reset calculation relates to the increasing use and societal vulnerability to *disinformation and disruptive technologies*. Modern societies are increasingly dependent on networked computer systems for a wide range of everyday activity. These systems are vulnerable to attack by nation states, terrorist organizations and other actors. Cyber attacks range from espionage (monitoring other countries to steal secrets), sabotage (stealing or destroying information), denial-of-service attacks, propaganda and disinformation to economic disruption (*eg* interfering with banks or payment systems). Cyber attacks muddy the boundaries of what constitutes war. They sow confusion and chaos.

Combat drones have become emblematic of a dangerous new era of warfare, and they have played a major role in the Ukraine war.[10] With a wingspan of 21 metres and the capacity to carry laser-guided missiles, the American Reaper

Drone is a proper aircraft and a serious weapon. But small-scale drones with deadly payloads can be relatively easily procured and assembled. 'Commercial drone technology is so widely available that anyone could build a crude DIY drone attack for a few hundred dollars and some terrorist groups have.'[11]

One could add to this worrying catalogue the threats posed by so-called 'drone swarms,' hypersonic missiles and fully autonomous weapons (or 'killer robots'). The world is becoming a very dangerous place. New weapons raise major new ethical challenges. Nation states are now spending vast sums on defence. [12] The growing economic and military influence of China is causing major new international realignment. And in an uncertain political climate a vast array of deadly weapons could be deployed deliberately, or invoked accidentally, by democratic states, authoritarian regimes or terrorist organizations.

All of this raises vital questions for Christian witness in the decade ahead.

- What does the gospel mean in a world of increased insecurities, with potential new wars, deepening old cleavages and crises that affect all levels of our societies?
- What is the prophetic role of the church as a voice calling for truth and justice within such a context?
- How do we prepare Christian people to steer through the chaos which may lie ahead and play constructive roles in our societies amidst these global challenges?
- What role can churches play to counter social threats, minimize escalation risks and support the resilience of our societies?
- Above all, how do we convey the urgent need for the world to realize its interconnectedness, fragility and deep need for peace?

4

Is This a Proxy War?

Opinion is sharply divided as to whether the war in Ukraine is a proxy war. President Putin and other Russian actors frequently allege that Ukraine is standing proxy for NATO, and many Western commentators seem happy to describe the conflict as a proxy war. However, Ukrainians are clear that this is a real war in which Ukraine is defending itself against a hostile invader, not a proxy war.[13] In formal and semantic terms, this is surely correct: Ukraine is not acting at the bidding of either the US or NATO: Ukraine and Russia are the principal parties in the conflict.

Nonetheless, the UK and other Western countries are deeply involved. The UK has been a European leader in giving political, diplomatic and humanitarian assistance to Ukraine. As the second largest donor after the US, it committed £2.3 billion in military assistance to Ukraine up until February 2023 and has pledged to match that assistance in 2023. The UK in addition hosted a training programme (Operation Interflex), with the aim of training 10,000 new and existing Ukrainian personnel within 120 days. The UK has recently committed to training Ukrainian fast jet pilots, albeit maintaining that combat fighter aircraft will not be provided, at least in the short term.[14]

Ukraine is not a NATO member, and the UK along with other NATO countries is therefore clear that it will not deploy troops on the ground in Ukraine. Neither will it impose a no-fly zone in Ukraine, as this would bring NATO into direct conflict with Russia.

- From an ethical perspective, what is entailed in supplying sophisticated arms to a neighbouring country and training their troops, but not actually supplying troops or fighting oneself?
- Precisely how much support should be given and what kinds of arms should or should not be supplied, given that wars that are supported from external sources usually last longer and entail more casualties than wars that simply involve the principal parties?
- How is proportionality to be maintained given the inexorable pressure from Ukraine to ramp up supply?
- And short of the Russians deciding to go home, or Ukraine being forced to surrender, when would we know that it is time to stop?

5 Theory and Practice

Biblical Approaches to War

Scripture does not speak in one voice about war. There are several strands of biblical witness which need to be read together in order to get a properly full, rich and textured picture. For instance, many think of the 'holy war' commands linked to conquest (*eg* Deut 7.1–6 and 20.10–18 and Joshua 6 and 8). But this is largely a minority strand, and one that is complex and debated. Alongside these texts are strands that command peace with and care for the stranger (Lev 19.33–34, Deut 10.19); strands that set clear limitations on violence and actions in war, including environmental impact (*eg* Deut 20.19–20); a consistent condemnation of violence in Wisdom literature (*eg* Prov 3.31; 12.20); complex narratives of the mix of personal and communal factors that lead to war; and a concern for the impact of war on combatants and civilians. The Book of Judges notably problematizes war. It starts by retelling some of the events of Joshua in a different light, and moves on to explore multiple forms of conflict and their complexity (so for example the morally troubling attack by the Danites on the emphatically peace-loving people of Laish in chapter 18), and their tendency to move ever deeper into violence, as well as the inability of violence to lead to long-lasting peace. The Book of Judges ends with the tragic and violent reality of the collapse of God's people into civil war.

Although there are ways of seeing pacifism at work in the biblical corpus, we generally see a pragmatic approach that takes conflict as a part of human reality (*eg* Eccl 3.8) and asks not *whether one should go to war, but* how one should go to war, and explores, in both law and narrative, what good conduct in conflict may look like, what limits there may be and how the manner of war shapes what comes next.

Whilst the biblical setting for war is primitive and hugely different from modern warfare, there are nevertheless some strong resonances with the concerns of today, relating for example to: types of weapons and technology and the imbalance of power they create; the eradication of whole cities and mass killings; propaganda and how one speaks about war (communication being central to the biblical text, including in thinking about war); and the role of leaders in war and peace.

One interesting biblical strand highlighted in the last few years concerns the concept of moral injury and how to effect the transition of combatants from war to peace. Some of the legal texts set out processes of cleansing and returning, with rituals that signify the sharing of responsibility for acts of war by entire communities (*eg* Num 31.13–24).

The impact of war on civilians is explored relentlessly, particular with regards to forced displacement (especially but not solely in the prophetic corpus), and sexual violence towards women as a weapon of war (the end of Judges 5 is striking in that regard).

Throughout the historical books and the prophets there is a focus on international relations and on the complexity of politics along with an exploration of how nations and people may apportion blame and try to make sense of conflict in their particular context. All of these sit within wider recurrent themes in the Old Testament which are often linked to war—the difficulty of finding socio-political systems that enable the flourishing of all; economic injustice and oppression; the inability of violence to achieve lasting peace; abuses of power in private and public settings; child abuse, domestic abuse and sexual violence; toxic masculinity and its links to patterns of violence; moral and religious confusion; the problem of pursuing a strong sense of national and ethnic identity and how this is nurtured over and against the 'other.'

The New Testament does not directly address the question of war. But it is very much concerned with the establishment of peace. In the New Testament, Jesus proclaims the dawning of the kingdom of God. The ethic of the new messianic age is characterized by meekness, righteousness, mercy and peacemaking (Matt 5.3–10). Going beyond the mere doing of justice, Jesus commands not just love of neighbour but also love of enemies (Matt 5.43–47). His followers are to meet injustice and even violence with forgiveness, prayer and blessings for the enemy together with attempts at reconciliation (Matt 5.38–42). All this is in continuity with the Old Testament, where the achievement of a just, righteous and peaceful life in community is depicted as the goal of the covenant between God and Israel and is expected to characterize the messianic age.

The early church sought to embody the ideal of a peaceful life in its community practices (Acts 4.32–37). St Paul exhorts his readers to be ministers of reconciliation (2 Cor 5). Christians are discouraged from taking out lawsuits against one another, let alone resorting to violence (1 Cor 6). Peace with God is understood as leading to peace with one another through the presence and indwelling of the Holy Spirit, who is the Spirit of peace. As he invokes this Spirit upon them, so Jesus prays for his followers to know a complete unity, living in the world whilst not being 'of' this world (John 17).

Theological Responses to War

The question of how the Christian community ought to manifest within itself the signs of the peaceable kingdom, whilst continuing to live in a world of injustice, violence and war generates tension. Christians responded to this tension in different ways.

Until AD 170–180 there is no direct evidence either that Christians participated in military service or that they abstained from it. For various reasons, including their position in society and their relation to the Roman Empire, it is likely that few Christians were soldiers. There is evidence that some Christians served in the army from AD 170, and their numbers grew over subsequent decades. The situation changed dramatically with the conversion of Constantine, and by AD 416 *only* Christians could serve in the army. Nevertheless, 'The age of persecution down to the time [of] Constantine was the *age of pacifism* to the degree that during this time no Christian author to our knowledge approved of Christian participation in battle.'[15]

The pacifist tradition was continued by groups in the radical reformation such as some of the Anabaptists. It has been common amongst members of historic peace churches, such as the Quakers, Mennonites and Brethren. Significant protestant pacifist theologians today include John Howard Yoder and Stanley Hauerwas. Two World Wars left Europe horrified and sickened by war, and in the last few decades, pacifism has become increasingly familiar in Roman Catholicism. Pope Francis's utterances on war are sometimes pacifist in tone. Thus,

> Three world wars in a single century! The one of 1914–1918, the one of 1939–1945, and this one!... That is why you, who are journalists, please be pacifists, speak out against wars, fight against war. I ask you as a brother. Thank you.[16]

Pacifism today takes different forms, depending on whether it is felt to be a distinctive moral obligation for members of the Christian community or whether it is pragmatically (and possibly also morally) thought to be the right posture for the whole body politic. In view of the great dangers posed by the profusion of new and dangerous weapons, this countercultural call to non-violence is surely urgently needed today.

The main Western Christian alternative to pacifism is the just war tradition. This was inaugurated with the writings of Ambrose of Milan and especially Augustine of Hippo in the fourth and fifth century. Augustine identified the reluctant and limited use of force as one of the ways in which a Christian might in love be required to serve the needs of an innocent neighbour under attack by an assailant. Augustine wrote out of a perceived need to defend the

Roman Empire (now a Christian state) from invading Germanic peoples. Just war tradition therefore historically came into being as a product of a close relation between church and wider society, and it has ever since developed in dialogue with the requirements of statecraft.[17] What have become the classical grounds for a just war were set out systematically by Thomas Aquinas as 'right authority, just cause and right intention.'[18] Other grounds (last resort, proportionality and reasonable prospect of success) have been included in the tradition over time. Contemporary exponents of the just war tradition include the Oxford ethicists Professor Oliver O'Donovan[19] and Professor Nigel Biggar.[20]

The war effort mounted by Ukraine and allies is understood, from a Western military perspective and more widely, to be justified from within the Western just war tradition. Given Putin's maximalist demands over Ukraine, the brutality that citizens of Ukraine overrun by Russia have experienced, and the real fears of further Russian expansion experienced by other countries in the region, Western military support is seen as ethically appropriate. Moreover, the supply of modern precision weapons by NATO is seen to have reduced casualties on both sides in the actual conduct of war, through an ability to strike logistic and command and control nodes, supply dumps and significant road and rail routes without the necessity always to target troops. Perhaps the area where the ethics of this tradition are the most stretched is in regard to proportionality, where it is not possible to see in the midst of the conflict whether or not the bloodshed becomes higher than it otherwise would have been from the gradually ramping up of weapons supply, or not.

Importantly, Eastern Orthodoxy has never subscribed to Western just war thinking. The experience and teaching of Orthodox Christianity do not fit neatly within the categories of pacifism, just war theory or holy war. Instead, they provide pastoral resources for the pursuit of a dynamic praxis of peace.[21] One Orthodox scholar summarizes as follows:

> Orthodoxy has neither a crusade ethic nor an explicit just war theory. Instead, the church tolerates war as an inevitable, tragic necessity for the protection of the innocent and the vindication of justice. Peace-making is the common vocation of all Christian, but the pursuit of peace in a corrupt world at times inevitably requires the use of force. In such circumstances, the church provides spiritual therapy for healing from the damaging effects of taking life. In every Divine Liturgy, the church prays for the peace of the world and all its inhabitants, and participates in the heavenly banquet of the kingdom, to which all—soldier and pacifist alike—are invited.[22]

The absence of just war thinking in Orthodoxy means that Western appeals to the just war tradition have little traction in dealings with Russia in this conflict.

6 Church, State and War

There is a religious dimension to the Russia-Ukraine war. According to a fairly recent Pew Research Center survey, religion in large parts of the post-communist East has converged with nationality in conferring personal and national identity. Thus, although rates of church attendance are not high, some 71% of Russians and 78% of Ukrainians identify as Orthodox Christians.[23] 'Russian world' thinking receives spiritual support and legitimacy from Russian Orthodox Church leadership. And the internal tensions within Ukraine are reflected in a split between a Constantinople-facing Orthodox Church of Ukraine and a Moscow-facing Ukrainian Orthodox Church.

The Church of England retains, via the office of the Archbishop of Canterbury, a link to the Russian Orthodox Patriarch. And the ROC remains a member of the World Council of Churches. These personal links and channels of communication are to be nurtured in so far as they provide a basis to engage with significant counterparties in Russia. This is important not just for dialogue about the search for peace now, but because the state of relationships between religious leaders within Ukraine and Russia will have a bearing on the nature of the peace achieved at the eventual end of the war.

The invasion of Ukraine has rightly been condemned by a wide range of religious leaders as illegal and unjustified. The willingness of UK citizens to support humanitarian, financial and military aid to Ukraine has been commendable. But the church has a role in continuing to express grief at the immense suffering caused by this conflict, to pray and work for a just peace and to resist any tendency either to glory in British achievements on the one hand or to demonize Russia on the other.

7

Loving Our Neighbour in the Context of War

At the heart of Christian faith and ethics is the dual command to love God and neighbour. This essentially Old Testament framework is endorsed and expanded by Jesus into love, not just for the neighbour but for the enemy, and it remains the heart of the law and the Christian life. It can be said that the purpose of Christ's coming was to enable us to become people capable of love for God and neighbour. In situations of war, however, what does it mean to love one's neighbour?

Jesus' Parable of the Good Samaritan centres on the question of the identity of the object of our love—'Who is my neighbour?' When war breaks out in some part of the world, the question inevitably is raised as to the responsibilities of neighbour love in this context.

Regarding war in Ukraine, where the UK is not directly involved, who is our neighbour? Is it Ukraine? Russia? And who is the 'our' in that sentence—the state or the church?

Throughout the Christian tradition there is a distinction made between the role of the church and the role of the state when it comes to war. So different, but overlapping, considerations inform the responsibility of the church and the nation state, when a neighbour is attacked.

The Role of the Church

The Samaritan in the story has been understood in several ways. In one reading, he is an image of Christ, who reaches down to the broken sinner or human race, to save and rescue, at cost to himself. This is not incompatible with another reading that takes the Samaritan as a picture of the calling of the church—to 'go and do likewise.'

One might take Origen as an example of patristic attitudes to war. Along with most early Christians, he argues that Christians should not fight in wars, because their role in the body politic is distinct and different. Just as pagan priests kept their right hand undefiled for the sake of the sacrifices and are not enlisted for war, the same should be true for Christians: 'Christians also should be fighting as priests as worshippers of God, keeping their right hands pure and by their prayers to God striving for those who fight in a righteous cause and for the emperor who reigns righteously in order that everything opposed and hostile to those who act rightly may be destroyed.'[24] Through the patristic era, and into medieval times and the Reformation, the primary responsibility of Christians in a time of war was usually understood as prayer, their stance being devoted primarily toward the kingdom of God rather than the political powers of the time. In the Russia-Ukraine conflict, the first thing that many of us did, and have continued to do, was to pray.

Athanasius goes further to argue that Christian faith has the capacity to soften the warlike qualities of people. He speaks of bellicose barbarians who 'when they hear the teaching of Christ, straightaway instead of fighting they turn to husbandry and instead of arming their hands with weapons they raise them in prayer, and in a word, in place of fighting among themselves, henceforth they arm against the devil and against evil spirits, subduing these by self restraint and virtue of soul.'[25]

This teaching is problematic in countries such as Russia and Ukraine where a majority of the population identify as Christian; nonetheless it does reiterate that the distinct role of the church in time of war is not only to pray, as Origen urges, but to seek to moderate the warlike instinct within the warring parties.

Furthermore, Augustine argues that 'The real evils in war are love of violence, revengeful cruelty, fierce and implacable enmity, wild resistance, and the lust of power, and such like.'[26]

The church, aware of the spiritual dimensions of conflict as much as its physical harm, can also recognize that as a similar neighbour in the Eurasian continent, Russia is also our neighbour in this time of war. The aggressor is assailed, not by attacks from outside but by the internal passions of violence, cruelty and enmity which do harm to the soul—reflected in the modern concept of 'moral injury.' This is particularly true for a nation such as Russia which understands itself as broadly Christian and where troops and weapons are blessed by the Orthodox Patriarch. Russia may critique the West for its decadence but needs to be reminded that spiritual battles are not fought with tanks and bullets.

Bishop George Bell put it very well when, in November 1939 and faced with a terrible impending European war, he said, *'It is the function of the church at all costs to remain the church.'*

The state has certain functions that are its proper remit in time of war including the defence of the realm, the conduct of foreign policy and decisions about whether and how to prosecute war. However, the proper remit of the church during time of war is the same as its remit during times of peace, namely the proclaiming of the gospel of salvation in word and in deed and the formation of disciples of Jesus Christ. At times of national crisis, national churches run the risk of being co-opted into the service of a national political vision. The leadership of the Russian Orthodox Church has, wrongly, done just that. In Ukraine too, it must be admitted, there is a confusing and sometimes toxic mixture of Orthodox religion with national political ideals. And there are risks that the Church of England could be co-opted into a broader agenda that provides uncritical support of the Ukrainian war effort. But the church's message is to follow Jesus Christ in announcing the coming of God's kingdom, to call for conversion of life, to celebrate the gift of divine grace, to pronounce the forgiveness of sins and to announce and enact a peace which comes from above. The church's task is to form disciples who live well and display the characteristics of the life of Christ wherever they are: civilians or combatants, directly involved in war, or involved in war at one remove.

The Role of the State

Origen, as well as Augustine, of course, recognizes that at times war is necessary, referring to 'those who fight in a righteous cause,' particularly in times of self defence—as is clearly the case for Ukraine. For the state, there remains the question of what it means to be a good neighbour when a neighbouring country has been attacked, as Ukraine has been.

The Samaritan's support for the neighbour consists of doing whatever they can to soften the impact of violence upon the victim and to aim at restoration. So, first, being a good neighbour must include practical relief efforts to support those who have lost home or health or well-being as a result of the war.

Secondly, to moderate warlike passions, such support could focus on diplomatic efforts to restrain the hand of the aggressor. One of the primary ways of supporting Ukraine must be to use whatever persuasive or economic means are possible to make the ongoing prosecution of the war difficult. This includes sanctions, economic and social consequences, to discourage the warlike impulse.

Thirdly, forms of military support may be seen as just and appropriate, an act of compassion for a neighbour under pressure of attack to enable them to defend themselves. Yet this should surely be under certain conditions. Support should enable self defence, rather than providing the means of mounting aggressive counter attacks. It should not provide the kind of weaponry that enables revenge or escalation of the war beyond what is necessary for self defence.

The Radical Witness of the Gospel

Perhaps especially for an established church, there is a risk that the distinctive role of the church can be elided by the role of the state, as church leaders are under pressure to speak in ways which make political sense and support the pragmatic achievement of results.

But the command to love our neighbours, to love the stranger, and even to love our enemies, is a radical commandment. Archbishop Tutu reflecting on Christian discipleship says:

> The church of God has to be the salt and light of the world. We are the hope of the hopeless, through the power of God. We must transfigure a situation of hate and suspicion, of brokenness and separation, of fear and bitterness. We have no option. God wants us to be the alternative society; where there is harshness and insensitivity, we must be compassionate and caring; where people are statistics we must show they count as being of immense value to God; where there is grasping and selfishness we must be a sharing community now.[27]

We live in a world of insiders and outsiders, a world where some are welcome and others are permanently shunned. We build barriers of ethnic and racial differences. We build barriers on the basis of economic, social or political differences. Barriers pop up when differences of gender, physical or mental ability, education or religion make us closed and inhospitable. Or we hide behind barriers on account of prejudice, grudges, unhealed hurts or painful memories. Instead of nurturing friendship and intimacy, we foster indifference, disconnection and strangement. We are experts at exclusion because we prefer the comfortable and familiar neighbour to the stranger whose presence may not just challenge us but even remake our world. Churches are not immune to this. We may not consciously construct these walls, in fact, we are probably hardly aware of them, but they are there. Most Christian congregations are fairly homogeneous. We feel comfortable only to talk to people we know, not the stranger.

- So imagine, for a moment, as a Christian, how do we respond to the stranger dying in a remote war?
- How do we avoid othering, dehumanizing and caricaturing the one seen as the enemy?
- In the context of the deeply fragmented and broken world order, how can we create Christian witness that does not mimic and mirror the discords, divisions and discriminations?

8 Imagining Tomorrow: Waging War and Preparing for Peace

At present neither side in the conflict is ready to negotiate, and recent history of conflicts indicates successful peace negotiations usually require a 'mutually hurting stalemate.' However, whilst this might be a psychological and historical reality, it is neither an ethical statement nor an inevitability, especially for Christians operating with the assumption of God's involvement in human affairs. Previous conflicts have shown that even where formal peace settlements remain elusive, truces and ceasefires are possible and can, as with Cyprus and the Korean peninsula, prove to be relatively durable. The church therefore should encourage by all means the imaginative creation of relationships and fora where negotiations could take place to bring the fighting to an end. We need to ask: in a conflict where fundamentally different value systems, ethical frameworks and readings of history are in play, where might shared values, interests and identities be found, and which actors might best be positioned to build a bridge across the divide?

Where might shared values, interests and identities be found

Numerous political initiatives are being proposed, most notably President Zelensky's 10-point peace plan. Peace plans have also been proposed by, for example, China, Brazil and South Africa. And private peace initiatives of various kinds are in train.

From a church perspective, the Archbishop of Canterbury visited Ukraine and met with a range of religious leaders in November/December 2022. The Conference of European Churches has launched a plan entitled 'Pathways to Peace.' Pope Francis has launched a peace mission aimed at finding a settlement. The World Council of Churches, which includes the Russian Orthodox Church (ROC) as its largest member, has convened meetings including both sides and has made official visits to Kyiv, meeting Ukrainian Orthodox Church (UOC) and Orthodox Church of Ukraine (OUC) leaders, and to Moscow, meeting Patriarch Kirill. At present, the WCC seems the most likely body to enable intra-Orthodox dialogue. One of the functions of the UK Churches could be to support any dialogue the WCC can achieve politically, and with human or financial resources.

There are many friendships with Russian Christians both in Russia and in the Russian diaspora, not least in the UK, that are to be treasured, especially with a view to the eventual and vital rebuilding of relationships *post bellum*.

The position on the war taken by the Russian regime, supported by the leadership of the ROC, needs to be distinguished from that of ordinary Russians and ordinary believers, many of whom (though by no means all) oppose the war and do not accept the official narrative. In our speech and actions we are to be careful of stereotyping and are to seek always to see the other as a full person not as a label or caricature. Outside Russia, Orthodox churches often bring Russians and Ukrainians together. The Church of England sometimes offers buildings to these communities for their worship. The Anglican Chaplain in Moscow, Malcolm Rogers, has maintained warm and strong relationships with ROC leaders for the last five years, albeit that he returned to the UK at the end of June 2023.

At a human level, the achievement of a just peace after so much blood has been spilt can seem almost impossible. But it is the church's task to hold out a bigger vision, to seek a peace which comes from above, and to remind everyone that 'With God nothing will be impossible.'

One of the particular contributions of the church is prayer. Christians have prayed faithfully and fervently for those caught up in the war. Note particularly the 'Prayers across Europe' for peace using Zoom-based gatherings for prayer and worship during Lent and Advent organized by the Diocese in Europe. Prayer expresses our lament for the tragedy of war. Prayer changes hearts and minds. Prayer invokes the action of a God whose longing for humankind is a peace that the world itself cannot give. And prayer changes the one who prays as we learn to see the world through God's eyes.

Prayer expresses our lament for the tragedy of war

The eventual cost of rebuilding Ukraine will be huge—the figure of one trillion dollars has been mooted. It is not too early for discussions to begin about how this money will be raised and deployed. There is surely some moral link between the supply of weaponry and the supply of finance and expertise to enable rebuilding when the weapons eventually fall silent. At the same time, the cost of reconstruction should not be calculated solely in economic terms and overlook the spiritual, mental and psychological costs of the war. The rebuilding of Ukraine will involve a major ethical and spiritual component: rebuilding trust, integrity, love and friendship through leadership that inspires the confidence that peace will be secure and Ukraine will emerge better and stronger. Ukrainians will need pastoral care. And soldiers on all sides will need rehabilitation from trauma and moral injury.

As the majority church, the Orthodox church will have an important part to play in this.

Ukraine has only recently developed a professional military chaplaincy. The Royal Army Chaplains Department has during summer 2023 trained a cohort of Ukrainian chaplains in Britain in the core elements of chaplaincy delivery—spiritual support, moral guidance and pastoral care—as well as spiritual resilience, holistic fitness and moral injury.

From a Christian perspective, the goal is an active, positive peace founded upon justice. Forty years ago, the Roman Catholic bishops of the USA expressed well this positive notion of peace in their Pastoral Letter *The Challenge of Peace:*

> Catholic teaching has always understood peace in positive terms. In the words of Pope John Paul II: 'Peace is not just the absence of war…Like a cathedral, peace must be constructed patiently and with unshakable faith' (Coventry, England, 1982). Peace is the fruit of order. Order in human society must be shaped on the basis of respect for the transcendence of God and the unique dignity of each person, understood in terms of freedom, justice, truth and love. To avoid war in our day we must be intent on building peace in an increasingly interdependent world.[28]

In these terms, a peaceful Ukraine is not the same as a state locked in a frozen conflict, such as we see in Korea, or, in a different way in Kashmir on the India/Pakistan border. The ultimate goal is reconciliation, the restitution of relationships and the creation of a social order that provides the best environment for the deep wounds to begin to heal.

- How can friendships with Russian Christians be maintained so as to keep to a minimum the negative effects on Russia-Western relations for the long term?
- How are parishes, dioceses and the nation to be resourced for continuing prayer for Ukraine?
- How will the global church and the UK churches support rebuilding? And how can we best help the two national Orthodox communities, currently seriously divided, in their leadership role in Ukraine?

9 Christian Witness in an Uncertain World

Walter Brueggemann has called for a re-awakening of the prophetic imagination characterized by three urgent prophetic tasks. Brueggemann considers the content of Old Testament prophecy generated around the cataclysmic fall of Jerusalem in BC 587 and is relating this to post-9/11 America. But the framework is of wider applicability. These three tasks seem an appropriate way to end this paper in the context of British involvement with the Ukraine-Russia war.

Reality Amidst Ideology

Dealing with Complexity

The situation in Ukraine is complex, involving a difficult and disputed history, a large geographical territory that embodies eastern and western-facing elements, different versions of national identity, alternative languages, multiple religious jurisdictions and huge trauma. How can we cope with this?

- There is a place for simply holding the situation before God and recognizing our own limitations and impunity. We cannot understand everything and we cannot solve the crisis. We can, however, trust that God knows, God loves and God understands.'
- Adopting a posture of humility and intelligent enquiry, listening to those most involved, building and maintaining relationships.
- Supporting the relevant international institutions, both secular and religious, and appreciating the extreme difficulty of their role.
- Reflecting on the rich scriptural material on war and peace, appreciating that it is equally deep and complex but also a source of divine insight.
- Holding on to a few basic ethical commandments: loving God, loving our neighbour, endeavouring to love our enemies, being people of peace.

Building Resilience

We are to be alert to the signs of the times. The world is increasingly defined by danger, disorder and division. Ukraine has drawn in NATO and Russia on opposite sides; but there are looming concerns about much bigger political, economic and even military conflict between China and the USA. With generally increased military expenditure, the balance between whether the UK is running on a peace economy or a war economy is shifting.

In the dangerous and unpredictable times which are now upon us there is the need for a new and deeper resilience.

- Being a church that is rooted and being built up in Christ, trusting in the God who holds all things together, strengthened with power through the Holy Spirit.
- Supporting one another through small groups, community service projects, continuing to urge people to return to corporate worship post-COVID-19.
- Developing personal spiritual strength and everyday discipleship through rules of life, patterns of prayer, meditation on Scripture.
- Emphasizing the development of the church as a community of Christ-like character and virtue (compare Eph 6.10–18) whilst resisting pressure to collude with therapeutic individualism and the cult of the self—being completely realistic about the power of this culture.
- Stressing irreducibility of love of God and neighbour as the basis for a viable and worthwhile life.
- Teaching the art of a good and happy life. Challenging the Western expectation of a happy life from which suffering is eliminated, whilst recovering the biblical vision (as given in the psalms) that hardship and struggle are endemic to the human condition, yet something to fight against through imagination, pursuit of justice, lament and interdependence.

Acknowledging Interdependence

- Acknowledging the deep and increasing interconnectedness of the planet—economically, environmentally, militarily and lamenting the way that these same relationships have become weaponized by the war.
- Renewing our commitment to ongoing ecumenical work towards reconciliation as a visible sign that bears witness to a divided humanity and anticipates the eschatologically-reconciled and united humanity that God intends to bring about in Christ.
- Renewing efforts to work for global justice, aware this is a foundation long term for true and lasting peace.

- Praying for the victims of the many conflicts that afflict our world.
- Giving thanks for the welcome given to Ukrainian refugees by the UK, whilst lamenting a more general culture of hostility to migrants.
- Bringing interdependence closer: supporting the close neighbour who struggles but also giving sacrificially and getting involved in community projects: the post-coronation 'Big Help Out' showed the possibilities at a national level.

Grief Amid Denial

The impact of the Ukraine-Russia war has already been appalling: hundreds of thousands of dead and injured; displacement of some eight million people; destruction of entire cities; an area the size of Britain contaminated by mines. Psychologically, we can respond to such terrible events either by shutting them out of our consciousness or else being overwhelmed by them. Through its worship, the church offers another way—the language of lament. Faced with a culture of denial, the church's function is to embrace, model and practice grief in order that these tragic losses can be acknowledged. Thus:

- Counter a persuasive post-Enlightenment narrative of scientific and technological progress which has insulated us from the physical pain that many of our forbears knew but which holds out an illusory promise of a world of ever-increasing human happiness.
- Recover the language of lament which is such a central part of our biblical inheritance (the Psalms, Job, Jeremiah, Lamentations, 2 Corinthians, the passion of Christ) but which frequently drops out of our worship. Restore a balance in worship between praise and lament—a particular issue for some charismatic / evangelical communities.
- Promote the kind of liberal education which includes serious engagement with those many parts of the world where mixing of ethnic groups and tribes, colonization, the historical ebb and flow of major powers tend to produce factors now leading to conflict and war.
- Learn from the practices and language of the Global South, such as spiritual music and song.
- Cultivate the awareness that it is lament which gives rise to the hope of transformation and the coming of justice and peace.

Hope Amid Despair

Contrary to the opinion of Sigmund Freud, religious believers do not take refuge in an illusory consolation as a refuge from the harsh realities of life.

Rather, they find a realism about their circumstances in which they linger with courage and in which they practise their faith in God.

Drawing richly on Old Testament prophecy, Brueggemann suggests that hope is a tenacious act of imagination given in dream, oracle, narrative and song, rooted in absolute authority concerning divine purpose. Hope is an act of playful imagination with ill-defined and open images that suggest without giving clarity. Hope is given in an imaginative way, because it is out beyond what we know. Hope is enacted with tenacity: the prophets defied experienced reality and settled authority in order to voice a new reality out beyond present arrangements. Hope is an audacious claim, said to be the very word of God, the word that 'will stand for ever' (Isa 40.8), the word that will 'accomplish that which I purpose' (Isa 55.11), the word that is 'fire in your mouth' (Jer 5.14) that cannot be held in (Jer 20.9).

For Christians, hope is rooted in the resurrection of our Lord Jesus Christ. In raising Jesus from the dead, God intervenes decisively in human affairs, bringing joy out of grief and light where there was deepest darkness. The resurrection of Jesus Christ is an anticipation of the last great day of resurrection when the end comes, the dead are raised and all rulers, authorities and powers are placed under God's own ordering rule (1 Corinthians 15). Christians look forward in hope to a new heaven and new earth when the nations will all walk by the light of the glory of God, and where there will be no more mourning or crying or tears. (Revelation 21).

In the situation of Ukraine, we may pray that prophets and poets will arise who can give eloquent and persuasive voice to the longing and hopes for justice and peace, for Ukrainian religious leadership that will declare with authority the voice of the Lord and articulate a compelling future vision. Meanwhile, Ukrainians we have encountered take heart from the miracles they have experienced, such as the halting of the Russian advance at Irpin, at the very gates of Kyiv and the turning around and return of the long convoy of tanks which threatened to encircle and storm the city. Many Ukrainian refugees have expressed their profound gratitude for the welcome and care they have received from host families across Europe. And the outpouring of support from many people, countries and churches gives reason to believe that love may yet overcome hatred and violence give way to a positive peace.

Notes

1 Article by Vladimir Putin, 'On the Historical Unity of Russians and Ukrainians,' President of Russia (kremlin.ru).
2 Article by G Faulconbridge, 'Putin casts war as a battle for Russia's survival,' Reuters, 26 Feb 2023.
3 Article by P Wintour, 'Russia's belief in Nato "betrayal"—and why it matters today,' The Guardian, 12 Jan 2022.
4 ibid.
5 'Cost of living crisis sees some people considering suicide,' BBC News, 12 March 2022.
6 'A World Divided: Russia, China and the West,' Bennett Institute for Public Policy (cam.ac.uk) 20 October 2022.
7 K Mehta, member of the Board of the American Committee for US Russia Accord and a Senior Global Justice Fellow at Yale University, 'The Ukraine War viewed from the Global South,' MR Online, originally published 22 February 2023.
8 'Doomsday Clock moves to 90 seconds to midnight, signaling more peril than ever,' NPR.
9 'What to know about the New START treaty after Russia's latest move on nuclear weapons,' CNN Politics.
10 'Combat drones: We are in a new era of warfare—here's why,' BBC News, J Marcus, 4 February 2022.
11 P Scharre, Director of Studies at the Center for New American Security, in article cited above.
12 According to the Stockholm International Peace Research Institute, global defence expenditure exceeded 2 trillion dollars for the first time in 2021; 2021 was the 7th consecutive year that global expenditure had increased. The 5 largest spenders were: US $801bn; China $293bn; India $76.6bn; UK $72bn; Russia $66bn.
13 'Expert Comment: This is no proxy war—Russia really invaded Ukraine,' University of Oxford.
14 'Military assistance to Ukraine since the Russian invasion,' House of Commons Library (parliament.uk).
15 R Bainton quoted in J Childress, 'Pacifism' in New Dictionary of Christian Ethics (London: Westminster, 1986) pp 446–448.
16 In-flight conversation with journalist Fatima Al Najem reported in Vatican News 6 November 2022, Pope Francis: 'Three world wars in one century: be pacifists!' Vatican News.
17 J Turner Johnson, 'Just War' in New Dictionary of Christian Ethics, op cit, pp 328–329.
18 Summa Theologiae: War (Secunda Secundae Partis, Q. 40) (newadvent.org).
19 O O'Donovan, The Just War Revisited (Cambridge University Press, 2012).
20 N Biggar, In Defence of War (Oxford University Press, 2013).
21 See the website of the Orthodox Peace Fellowship, Incommunion.org, 'In Communion Journal,' Orthodox Peace Fellowship.
22 P LeMasters, 'Orthodox Perspectives on Peace, War and Violence,' Ecumenical Review (Geneva: World Council of Churches, 2011).
23 'Religious Belief and National Belonging in Central and Eastern Europe,' Pew Research Center.
24 Origen, Contra Celsum VIII.73.
25 Athanasius, De incarnatione Verbi Dei, p 52.
26 Augustine, 'Reply to Faustus,' NPNF 4, p 301.
27 D Tutu, The Voice of One Crying in the Wilderness (London: Mowbray, 1982) p 31.
28 Microsoft Word, The Challenge of Peace.doc (usccb.org) p 1.